My First Book about Jesus

Carine

CF4•K

© Copyright 2009 Carine Mackenzie
ISBN: 978-1-84550-463-2
Reprinted 2011 and 2014

Published by Christian Focus Publications,
Geanies House, Fearn,
Ross-shire, IV20 1TW,
Scotland, U.K.

The scripture quotations in this book are based on
the New King James version of the scriptures.

www.christianfocus.com
email:info@christianfocus.com

Cover design by Daniel van Straaten
All illustrations by Diane Mathes

Printed and bound by
Bell and Bain, Glasgow

MIX
Paper from
responsible sources
FSC® C007785

Contents

From the Author

Jesus has a great care for children. 'Let the children come to me,' he told his disciples. 'Don't forbid them.'

Jesus wants children today to come to him. Those with a responsibility for children should do all they can to tell them about Jesus the Saviour.

My prayer is that children will learn about Jesus, the Son of God, in this little book. It gives a brief outline of Jesus' life and work.

The text on each page is part of a longer story which would be well worth reading with your child.

Jesus' prayer in John 17 tells us how important it is to know him. 'This is life eternal that they may know you, the only true God, and Jesus Christ whom you have sent.'

Carine Mackenzie

Birth and Childhood

John 1:1

In the beginning was the Word, and the Word was with God, and the Word was God.

Jesus Christ is God the Son from all eternity. He is also called the Word of God. He became a man, born into this world, but he never stopped being God the Son. This is an amazing mystery for us to believe and cause us to worship.

Matthew 1:23

Behold, the virgin shall be with child, and bear a son, and they shall call his name *Immanuel*, which means, 'God with us'.

Jesus' birth was unique. He had a human mother, Mary. She conceived the baby, Jesus, by the power of God the Holy Spirit.

The special name 'Immanuel' means 'God with us.' Jesus was truly a human like us, but he was also truly God.

Luke 2:7

Mary gave birth to her firstborn son and wrapped him in swaddling cloths, and laid him in a manger, because there was no room for them in the inn.

Jesus' birth was in very humble surroundings. Mary and her husband Joseph could not find shelter at the inn. Jesus' first bed was the animals' feeding trough.

Matthew 1:21

You shall call his name *Jesus*, for he will save his people from their sins.

Joseph, Mary's husband, was a good man. An angel spoke to him in a dream and told him to call the baby JESUS, which means Saviour.

All sinful thoughts, words and deeds deserve God's punishment. Jesus would take that punishment himself and so be a Saviour for his people.

Luke 2:11,16

The angel said to the shepherds, 'There is born to you this day in the city of David a Saviour, who is Christ the Lord.'

...They hurried off and found Mary and Joseph, and the baby who was lying in the manger.

The angels told some ordinary shepherds at their work the wonderful news about the birth of Jesus Christ, the Saviour promised long ago. They rushed to see him and then passed on the good news to everyone they met.

Matthew 2:11

When the wise men had come into the house, they saw the young child with Mary his mother, and fell down and worshipped him. They presented gifts to him: gold, frankincense and myrrh.

Gold is a gift fit for a king. Jesus is a king who rules over his people. Frankincense is a perfume used by priests. Jesus is our great Priest, who sacrificed himself for us and always prays for us.

Myrrh was ointment used to anoint dead bodies. Jesus came to this world to die for his people.

Luke 2:42

When Jesus was twelve years old, they went up to Jerusalem according to the custom of the feast.

The special feast that Jesus attended was the Passover feast. This celebrated the night when the Israelites in Egypt painted lambs' blood on their doorposts. The 'angel of death' then passed over their homes and the Israelites were saved.

This event points to the greater salvation when Jesus shed his blood on the cross for sinners.

Luke 2:52

Jesus increased in wisdom and stature, and in favour with God and men.

Jesus showed obedience to his parents and obedience to God. He had no sin and so never did, said or thought wrong things like we do.

If we have faith in Jesus Christ, not only is our sin forgiven, but we are accepted by God not because we are good, but because Jesus was good for us.

Miracles

Mark 2:5

When Jesus saw their faith, he said to the paralytic, 'Son, your sins are forgiven you.'

Jesus has power to forgive sins because he is God. The teachers of the law were right when they said only God can forgive sins. To prove his power and authority over sin, Jesus also healed the man's body.
He was able to get up
and walk.

Luke 4:40

When the sun was setting, all those who had any that were sick with various diseases brought them to Jesus; and he laid hands on every one of them and healed them.

At the end of a busy day preaching and teaching, Jesus still took time to help sick and needy people. Jesus has power over illness because he is God.

Jesus has power and authority over all creation. He has power over death and sin. There is no one more powerful than the one true God: God the Father, Son and Holy Spirit.

Mark 1:40

A man with leprosy came to Jesus and begged him on his knees, 'If you are willing, you can make me clean.'

A person with leprosy had to leave his home and family because the disease was so dreadful. Nobody wanted to go near a leper. Jesus showed great kindness to this man by reaching out and touching him. Jesus was not only willing, but able to heal him from the terrible disease.

Mark 4:39

He got up, rebuked the wind and said to the waves, 'Peace! Be still!' Then the wind ceased and there was a great calm.

God created everything with a word – God created the wind and the sea with a word. Jesus (who is God the Son) spoke to the wind and the sea that he had created and they obeyed him.

Mark 5:41-42

Jesus took the child by the hand, and said to her, 'Little girl, I say to you, arise.' Immediately the girl arose and walked.

Jesus, the Creator of life, had power to restore life to the little girl. He has power even over death because he is God.

Luke 8:35

They came to Jesus, and found the man from whom the demons had departed, sitting at the feet of Jesus, clothed and in his right mind.

The man had lots of evil spirits from Satan living in him which made him behave in a strange way. People were afraid of him. When Jesus healed him, there was a big change in his behaviour.

Jesus is more powerful than Satan because He is God.

Matthew 14:19

Jesus took the five loaves and two fish, and looking up to heaven, he blessed and broke and gave the loaves to the disciples; and the disciples gave them to the people.

Jesus is concerned about every detail of our lives. He did not want the people to go away hungry. He has power to provide all that we need, because he is God.

John 2:5

Mary said to the servants at the wedding, 'Whatever he says to you, do it.'

Mary knew that Jesus was the Son of God. When the servants obeyed Jesus, the water in the big pots was changed into wine. Jesus has power over all creation because he is God.

Teaching

Luke 4:43

Jesus said, 'I must preach the kingdom of God to the other cities also, because for this purpose I have been sent.'

Jesus performed many amazing miracles – healing people, making blind men see, making water into wine, stilling the sea and lots more – but everywhere he went he wanted to preach about God and his kingdom.

Sinners need to hear the good news of Jesus Christ. It is only through trusting in him and his death on the cross, that we can be given eternal life.

21

Matthew 4:17

Jesus began to preach and to say, 'Repent, for the kingdom of heaven is at hand.'

Jesus tells us to repent – that is to turn from our sinful ways with sorrow and to turn to God wanting to love and serve him. Repentance is a gracious gift from our merciful God.

Matthew 7:28-29

When Jesus had ended these sayings, the people were astonished at his teaching, for he taught them as one having authority.

The people who heard Jesus speak knew that he spoke with great power. He is the mighty Lord. People knew by his words that he was in charge.

Luke 8:4-5

When a large crowd had gathered and people had come to him from every city, He told this parable, 'A sower went out to sow his seed...'

A parable is a story about everyday activities. Jesus told many parables to the people. These stories had hidden meanings about God's kingdom. Only those who trusted and believed in God would understand their true meaning.

We need to ask God to save us from our sin and to reveal the truth to us in the Bible.

Matthew 22:37-39

Jesus replied, 'Love the Lord your God with all your heart, with all your soul, and with all your mind.' This is the first and greatest commandment. And the second is like it. 'Love your neighbour as yourself.'

Jesus sums up the Ten Commandments with one word – love. If we love God with all our being then we will worship only him, not idols. We will give honour to his name and keep his day holy.

Loving others is shown by honouring our parents, and caring for the life, purity and property of others. We will also be truthful and content.

Prayer

John 17:20-21

I pray for those who will believe in me through their word; that they all may be one, as you, Father, are in me, and I in you.

Jesus prayed often to his Father but these prayers are not recorded for us. John in his Gospel tells us one of Jesus' prayers.

He prays for himself, he prays for his disciples and he prays for all believers through the centuries until today. He prays that we will be united in him.

Luke 6:12

Jesus went out to the mountain to pray, and continued all night in prayer to God.

Jesus had twelve special disciples whom he chose from his followers. Before he chose them, he prayed all night to God his Father. He knew it was an important decision.

We should also pray to God before making decisions. God has promised to help and guide us.

Matthew 14:23

He went up on the mountain by himself to pray. When evening came, he was there alone.

After feeding the five thousand, Jesus sent the crowds away. He told the disciples to sail across the lake, then he went to be alone, to pray to God his Father.

Prayer is important. Jesus recognised this. We need to speak to God our Father. We need to ask him to forgive us for our sins, to help us in our daily lives. But we also need to thank him and tell him that we love him.

Mark 1:35

Very early in the morning while it was still dark, Jesus got up and went to a solitary place, where he prayed.

Jesus got up early in the morning so that he could get peace to pray to his Father. Crowds of people were looking for him, but he went on to another town to preach.

It is important to pray to God, one to one. We need peace and quiet to talk to our Heavenly Father. We need to say sorry for the bad things in our lives. We need to ask God for his strength to defeat sin.

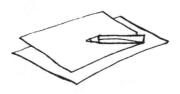

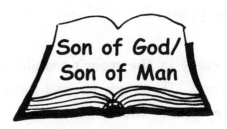

Son of God/
Son of Man

Luke 19:10

For the Son of Man has come to seek and to save that which was lost.

We all need God's salvation – we all disobey God's law and do wrong things. Jesus is powerful enough to change us because he is God. He died to take the punishment for our sins.

John 1:29

John the Baptist said, 'Behold! The Lamb of God who takes away the sin of the world!'

John was pointing to Jesus the Saviour. Jesus died on the cross as a sacrifice for the sins of his people. If we have faith in Jesus, he will take away our sin and make us clean in God's sight.

John 6:68-69

Peter answered, 'Lord, to whom shall we go? You have the words of eternal life. We believe and know that you are the Christ, the Son of the living God.'

Peter knew that Jesus is the one that we can safely trust. Peter showed that he had faith in Jesus, the Holy One of God.

It is only through Jesus that we can go to heaven when we die.

John 3:16

For God so loved the world that he gave his only begotten Son, that whoever believes in him should not perish, but have everlasting life.

God has given us many gifts, but the greatest one of all is the gift of his Son who came to this world as a man and willingly gave his life for us on the cross at Calvary. Jesus died in our place.

If we trust in the Lord Jesus, we have eternal life.

Mark 1:11

A voice came from heaven, 'You are my beloved Son, in whom I am well pleased.'

When Jesus was baptised in the River Jordan, the Spirit of God came down on him in the form of a dove. God the Father spoke from heaven. He was pleased with Jesus, God the Son. The Bible tells us that the Father is God, the Son is God, and the Spirit is God. The Bible also tells us that these three persons form only one God.

Matthew 8:20

Jesus said, 'Foxes have holes and birds of the air have nests, but the Son of Man has nowhere to lay his head.'

Jesus was born in a humble condition. He was poor. He did not own a house or have lots of money. Yet he is the Creator of the whole earth. He is the King of kings and Lord of lords. He became poor so that one day his people would have the riches and treasures of eternal life.

'I am'
Sayings

John 6:35

Jesus said, 'I am the bread of life. Whoever comes to me shall never hunger, and he who believes in me shall never thirst.'

Everyone has a longing that needs to be satisfied. This longing is like hunger or thirst. Our spirits or souls long for something that the world cannot give us. Money cannot buy satisfaction. Friends and family can't give it to us. The only satisfaction for this longing is in the Lord Jesus Christ.

John 8:12

Jesus said, 'I am the light of the world. Whoever follows me shall not walk in darkness, but have the light of life.'

Jesus as the light gives us guidance and leading. He clears away the darkness of evil. Jesus' light shows up our own sins and helps us to see him as our Saviour who takes away our sin.

John 10:11

Jesus said, 'I am the good shepherd. The good shepherd gives his life for the sheep.'

Jesus loves and cares for all those who follow him. He provides for their needs just as a good shepherd looks after his sheep. He loves his people so much that he even gave his life for them.

John 14:6

Jesus said, 'I am the way, the truth and the life. No one comes to the Father except through me.'

There is only one way to come to God and to be in heaven at last. That way is through the Lord Jesus Christ. All that Jesus says is true because he is truth. He is Creator of life and keeps us in life. Through him we can have eternal life in heaven.

Those who trust in him and believe that he is the only one who can save people from their sin, will one day be in heaven with Jesus forever.

John 10:9

Jesus said, 'I am the door. If anyone enters by me, he will be saved.'

To enter a room, we go through the door. Only through Jesus do we have access to God the Father, and have salvation from our sins.

John 15:5

Jesus said, 'I am the vine, you are the branches. Whoever abides in me, and I in him, bears much fruit.'

The branch which bears the grapes depends on the vine tree. If it is cut off from the vine it will die. Those who trust in Jesus depend on him for nourishment and life. A fruitful vine grows grapes. A fruitful Christian will show love, joy and peace.

John 11:25

Jesus said, 'I am the resurrection and the life. He who believes in me, though he may die, he shall live.'

Jesus has power over life and death. He rose from the dead and at the resurrection day believers will be raised up by him, to everlasting life.

The Cross

Matthew 26:26

While they were eating, Jesus took bread, blessed and broke it, and gave it to the disciples saying, 'Take, eat, this is my body.'

The Lord's Supper is still celebrated in Christian churches. The broken bread tells about Jesus' body which was crucified for his

people and the poured out wine tells of his blood which was shed for sinners.

Matthew 26:36

Then Jesus came with his disciples to a place called Gethsemane, and he said to them, 'Sit here while I go over there and pray.'

Jesus and his disciples often met in the garden of Gethsemane. Jesus was very sad. He knew what great suffering he would soon have when the anger of God was poured out on him. Jesus willingly took this anger on himself to save his people from suffering it.

Mark 15:22,25

They brought Jesus to the place called Golgotha... and they crucified him.

Jesus' suffering and death were part of a wonderful plan of salvation for his people. All sin deserves to be punished. Jesus took the full weight of the just anger of God on himself so that those who put their trust in him would be saved. Are you trusting in him?

Luke 23:34

Jesus said, 'Father, forgive them, for they do not know what they are doing.'

Even in the middle of his sufferings, Jesus prayed for those who were hurting him. He asked God to forgive them. What love he showed to his enemies! We should understand that we need forgiveness.

Mark 15:37,39

Jesus cried out with a loud voice, and breathed his last.

...When the centurion, who stood opposite Jesus, heard his cry and saw how he died, he said, 'Truly this man was the Son of God.'

The soldiers who witnessed Jesus' death were afraid. They were convinced that Jesus was truly the Son of God.

The Bible says that one day every knee shall bow and every tongue shall confess that Jesus Christ is Lord.

Mark 15:46

Joseph of Arimathea bought some fine linen, took Jesus down, wrapped him in the linen and laid him in a tomb cut out of the rock.

Joseph was a wealthy man who owned a burying place cut into the rock. The tomb was then sealed with a large round stone slab across the entrance.

Jesus was definitely dead. He wasn't pretending. He had died just as God had planned. But God's plan didn't end there.

Resurrection/
Ascension

Matthew 28:5-6

The angel said to the women, 'Do not be afraid, for I know that you are looking for Jesus, who was crucified. He is not here; he has risen.'

The Lord Jesus Christ conquered death. His body did not remain in the tomb. When the women came to see the tomb, the stone had been rolled away. Jesus was no longer there. He was alive again.

Sin and death had been conquered. Jesus showed God's power. There is no one more powerful than the one true God.

Luke 24:36

While the disciples were talking, Jesus himself stood among them and said to them, 'Peace be with you.'

Jesus appeared to many people after he rose from the dead. He came to the room where the disciples were meeting. They were frightened because they thought he was a ghost. He reassured them that he was really alive. He told them to touch him to make sure.

Are you one of those who believe in Jesus' resurrection?

Luke 24:51

While he blessed them, he left them and was carried up into heaven.

Jesus' body was taken up into heaven while the disciples watched. They worshipped him because he is God. They were filled with joy, praising and blessing God.

The Second Coming

Acts 1:11

This same Jesus, who was taken up from you into heaven, will so come in like manner as you saw him go into heaven.

God tells us that Jesus will come back to this earth. Everybody will bow before Jesus one day – either in judgement or trusting in him

by his gracious mercy. For God is truly gracious – because he loves us and offers salvation to his people who don't deserve his goodness.

Today

Hebrews 4:14

We have a great high priest, who has passed into the heavens, Jesus the Son of God.

A priest offers a sacrifice for the sins of the people. Jesus offered himself as the perfect sacrifice once and for all. A priest also prays for the people. Jesus in heaven is praying continually for his people.

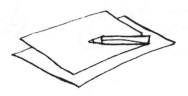

Acts 4:12

There is salvation in no other, for there is no other name under heaven given among men by which we must be saved.

Jesus Christ is the only way to God. Because he died and rose again, he is the Saviour for all who trust in him.

1 Timothy 2:5

For there is one God and one mediator between God and men, the man Christ Jesus.

Jesus is the only one who can make peace between a holy God and sinful men. He is both God and man. He became one of us and took our punishment. He never stopped being God. God the Father accepted his sacrifice for us.

Acts 5:31

God has exalted Jesus to his right hand to be Prince and Saviour, to give repentance to Israel and forgiveness of sins.

Jesus our Saviour is now exalted in heaven, sitting at God's right hand. Among his gifts to his people are repentance and forgiveness for all our sins.

Hebrews 7:25

Therefore he is able to save completely those who come to God through him, since he always lives to make intercession for them.

Sometimes we forget to pray for ourselves, but Jesus never forgets to pray for his people. He is always praying for them every day. That's what the word 'intercession' means.

Matthew 28:20

Jesus said, 'I am with you always, even to the end of the age.'

One of Jesus' names is Immanuel – 'God with us.' Jesus promised to be with his people always.

If you trust him, he is with you today and forever. He will never leave you.

John 20:31

These are written that you may believe that Jesus is the Christ, the Son of God, and that believing you may have life in his name.

The Gospel has been given to us by God so that we would come to know the Lord Jesus Christ and believe in him. Believing in him is the only way for us to be saved from sin and live a worthwhile life.

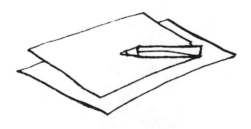

John 4:42

We believe, for we ourselves have heard him and we know that this is indeed the Christ, the Saviour of the world.

Some Samaritan men heard how one lady had met Jesus and he had changed her life. They heard Jesus themselves and then they believed that he was the Christ, the Saviour of the world.

You have also heard about Jesus. Do you believe in him? Is he your Saviour?

Memory record

Tick each book once you have learned each verse about Jesus. There are 56 of them.

1		12		23	
2		13		24	
3		14		25	
4		15		26	
5		16		27	
6		17		28	
7		18		29	
8		19		30	
9		20		31	
10		21		32	
11		22		33	

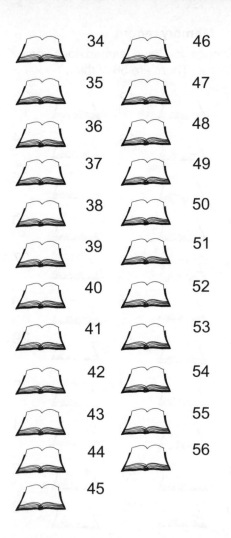

34

46

35

47

36

48

37

49

38

50

39

51

40

52

41

53

42

54

43

55

44

56

45

MY FIRST BOOK SERIES

My 1st Book of Bible Prayers, Philip Ross
ISBN: 978-1-85792-944-7

My 1st Book of Bible Promises, Carine Mackenzie
ISBN: 978-1-84550-039-9

My 1st Book of Christian Values, Carine Mackenzie
ISBN: 978-1-84550-262-1

My 1st Book of Memory Verses, Carine Mackenzie
ISBN: 978-1-85792-783-2

My 1st Book about the Church, Carine Mackenzie
ISBN: 978-1-84550-570-7

My 1st Book of Questions and Answers,
Carine Mackenzie
ISBN: 978-1-85792-570-8

My 1st Book about Jesus, Carine Mackenzie
ISBN: 978-1-84550-463-2

My 1st Book about the Bible, Carine Mackenzie
ISBN: 978-1-78191-123-5

My 1st Book about God, Carine Mackenzie
ISBN: 978-1-78191-260-7

My 1st Book about the Gospel, Carine Mackenzie
ISBN: 978-1-78191-276-8

CHRISTIAN FOCUS PUBLICATIONS

Christian Focus | Christian Heritage | CF4K | Mentor

Christian Focus Publications publishes books for adults and children under its four main imprints: Christian Focus, CF4K, Mentor and Christian Heritage. Our books reflect our conviction that God's Word is reliable and Jesus is the way to know him, and live for ever with him.

Our children's publication list includes a Sunday School curriculum that covers pre-school to early teens, and puzzle and activity books. We also publish personal and family devotional titles, biographies and inspirational stories that children will love.

If you are looking for quality Bible teaching for children then we have an excellent range of Bible stories and age-specific theological books.

From pre-school board books to teenage apologetics, we have it covered!

Find us at our web page:
www.christianfocus.com

CF4 •K
Because you're never too young to know Jesus